BIG SISTER LEARNS
ALL ABOUT BABIES [1]

Itty bitty newborn
(0-3 months)

WRITTEN BY **POLLY ZIELONKA**

ILLUSTRATED BY **MARIA KIRSHINA**

Dedication

To my two babies: You will not be babies for long.
Watching you grow every day is challenging and amazing,
all at once.

This is Claire. She just became a big sister to her baby brother, Eddie.
She is learning all about babies.

Baby Eddie is very tiny, so Claire makes sure to be
gentle with him. She tickles and kisses his toes,
and puts on a show for him.

He is not able to hold his toys yet,
but he likes to look at them.

"Shhhh....baby brother is sleeping."
Claire quietly watches him as he sleeps.

Baby has lots of growing to do,
which means he needs lots of sleep,
lots of milk, and lots of cuddles.

When baby Eddie sleeps, Claire has quiet playtime with her mommy and daddy. They color and do puzzles, but her favorite thing to do is build with blocks.

"Oh no, baby is crying!"

Claire's mommy explains that babies are not able to talk yet,
so this is Eddie's only way of letting them know
when he needs something...

...maybe he needs milk?

...maybe his tummy is bothering him?

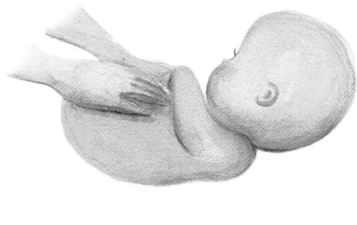

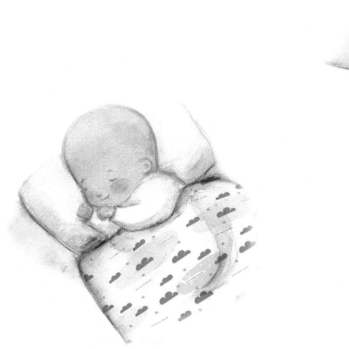

....or maybe it's time for a nap.

Sometimes Claire helps to calm him down by singing
sweet lullabies.

Baby Eddie tries to talk to Claire.
He coos and makes baby noises.
She lets him know she's listening by cooing back to him.

As baby Eddie gets bigger, he smiles when Claire puts on a show for him.
He watches everything she does!

Claire also helps baby with tummy time by putting toys in front of him. This helps him get stronger, so he can hold his head up on his own.

When he gets a little bigger, he will be able to sit up without any help.

Baby Eddie needs to visit the doctor
so they can make sure he's growing well.

The doctor tells Claire to wash her hands
before she plays with baby Eddie. They have to be careful
not to share any germs with him, so he does not get sick.

Some days Claire feels frustrated.
It can be hard work having a baby brother.
He needs a lot of care and attention.

Claire's mommy says she understands it can be difficult.
She gives Claire extra cuddles. Then Claire snuggles with her
teddy until she feels ready to play again.

Baby Eddie's favorite time is when Claire lays down
next to him to read books before bedtime.

But Claire has to watch out, baby wriggles everywhere!
He's still learning how to control his arms and legs.

Claire gives baby a little kiss on top of his head and says goodnight.

Then she snuggles up for her bedtime!

Made in the USA
Las Vegas, NV
12 February 2023

67396634R00017